The Powerful
PRAYER
of JABEZ

and Other
Life-Changing Prayers

Written by Randy Petersen

Illustrations by Elizabeth Mowry

n e w   s e a s o n s™
a division of Publications International, Ltd.

Randy Petersen is a graduate of Wheaton College with a degree in Ancient Languages. He is a full-time freelance writer and editor and has contributed to more than twenty books, including the *Revell Bible Dictionary* and the *Christian Book of Lists*. He has also contributed to a variety of magazines and is co-author of the book *Jesus: His Life and Times*.

Picture Credits:
Cover illustration: Elizabeth Mowry
Illustrations: Elizabeth Mowry; SuperStock: Christie's Images; Charles Neal.

Louis Weber, CEO
Publications International, Ltd.
7373 North Cicero Avenue
Lincolnwood, Illinois 60712

Manufactured in China.

8 7 6 5 4 3 2 1

ISBN: 0-7853-6318-1

Library of Congress Control Number: 2001095714

Contents

Pray as You Go

Hundreds of thousands of people have seen their spiritual lives transformed as they became aware of an obscure Old Testament character and his prayer. Jabez appears in only a sliver of 1 Chronicles, but he's there long enough to ask God for a few favors.

It's exciting to see people excited by prayer. Of course, the Bible is full of prayers, from Cain's plea for mercy to the final Hallelujah. That's what this book is about: using examples from Scripture to explore ways to communicate with God. The chosen prayers are offered in the hope that you'll use them in your life.

What It Is

What makes a prayer? Does it have to use special language? No. Does it have to occur in a religious setting? No, most of the prayers in this book didn't. Does it have to be a request? No, many prayers praise God.

Prayer is really just talking to God. And while some biblical prayers use lofty language to honor our Creator, many are rather casual. God is a real person, and he was treated that way by many of the most famous biblical characters. Abraham bargained with him, Moses complained to him, Samuel questioned him. Some of our examples are combinations of teaching and praying, talking *about* God as well as *to* him. Many folks in the Bible moved easily between prayer and conversation.

CHOOSE IT AND USE IT

THERE ARE different types of prayers in this book: prayers of praise, prayers for help and growth, even prayers of questioning. We can turn to God in good times and bad, even if we're not sure he's listening. Wherever you happen to be in your spiritual life, you can find a prayer in this book that comes close to expressing your thoughts and feelings. That's why we've included a "How to Pray This" section after each entry. This isn't just a book you read; it's a book you *use*. Use it to break new ground in your communication with God. Use it to jump-start a stalled relationship with God. Use it to come even closer to the Lord you love. Use it.

CHAPTER ONE

THREE ESSENTIAL PRAYERS

THE POWERFUL
PRAYER OF JABEZ
1 Chronicles 4:10

O H THAT YOU would bless me
and enlarge my border, and
that your hand might be with
me, and that you would keep me
from hurt and harm!

THE UNCOVERING OF JABEZ

A LL WE KNOW about Jabez comes from two
verses in 1 Chronicles, one of the Old
Testament's history books. This chronicle of
Israel's history begins with several chapters of
names—genealogies that start with Adam and
continue through all the kings of Judah. It
contains important biographical data but may
not be the most interesting reading matter.

All of a sudden in chapter 4, the list of
names stops, and we learn about an interesting man. "Jabez was honored more than his
brothers." We aren't told why he was hon-

ored, but throughout this history book the Chronicler draws a close connection between success and one's relationship with God. If Jabez received greater honor, it's likely that he was on good terms with his Creator.

The name Jabez is a pun on the word *pain*. We're told that his mother named him. Given the pain of childbirth, it's surprising that there weren't more children named Jabez. It's curious that he was named by his mother, since naming was often the father's right. In fact, there's no mention of his father at all, which causes us to wonder if the father had died shortly before his birth (providing another reason for the name "Pain").

This is speculation, of course, since the Bible tells us so little. But we do have a parallel story in Genesis. Jacob's beloved wife Rachel died while bearing Benjamin, and so Benjamin was honored more than his brothers, along with Joseph, Rachel's other son. Both Joseph and Benjamin carried the honor of being living reminders of a dead spouse. Maybe Jabez did, too.

Understanding the Prayer

AFTER WE MEET Jabez and learn the circumstances of his birth, we hear his prayer. There are four main things he prays for: blessing, enlarged borders, God's helping hand, and protection.

First, he asks God to **bless** him. This word is used hundreds of times in the Old Testament, and God is usually the subject of the verse. The first chapter of the Bible tells us that God blessed the first humans and told them to "be fruitful and multiply" (Genesis 1:28). Later, God blessed Noah and Abraham, promising to "bless those who bless you" (Genesis 12:3).

But what is blessing? To bless is to make good things happen for someone or to wish for or speak those good things. When God is doing the blessing, the wishing, speaking, and making are all wrapped up together. Jabez wanted a good life, a life that would be pleasing to God.

Next, Jabez asks God to **enlarge his border**. He wanted more land. In an agrarian society like ancient Israel, more land meant more wealth, but also more responsibility. We're not even sure when Jabez lived, but his request makes us think it was during the time when the Israelites were settling in the land of Canaan. Land was being allotted tribe by tribe, clan by clan, family by family. Jabez wanted as much as he could get. It would take some effort to develop and farm a large plot, but he was able to meet the challenge.

Don't pray this prayer looking to get rich. That's not what Jabez's prayer was about. Pray for enlarged opportunities to serve the Lord. Ask for a new awareness of your gifts and new chances to use them. Ask for sensitivity to the needs of those around you.

Third, Jabez prays that **God's hand might be with him**. The hand of God was (and is) a source of strength and guidance. Think of an actual hand pushing, lifting, pointing, and leading you. That's what God's hand does throughout Scripture. Jabez knew he needed that support every step of the way.

This is a prayer that's guaranteed to be answered affirmatively. God has promised to be with us. "I will never leave you or forsake

you," he says (Hebrews 13:5). We might go through times when his presence is less obvious than usual, but he's always there for us.

Finally, Jabez asks for **protection from hurt and harm**. He actually uses the Hebrew word that sounds like his name. It's possible that he doesn't want to be hurt or *cause* hurt. Or he might be talking about short-term pain and long-term damage. Or physical injury and spiritual injury. Or maybe he just uses two words for the same thing. In any case, he wants God's protective shield.

God has never promised us a life free from pain. In fact, Jesus said, "In the world you face persecution" (John 16:33). But we certainly can ask for God's protection, especially if that means we'll be able to "enlarge our borders"—that is, expand our ministry.

If Jabez was involved in the settlement of Canaan, then enlarging his borders might have meant doing battle with the Canaanites. In that case, he was asking for God's blessing on the endeavor, God's empowering hand, and safety in the struggle. If we apply that to our efforts to live more fully for Christ, it might mean stepping outside our comfort zone and becoming more vulnerable to all sorts of injuries—physical, spiritual, emotional, relational, etc. We should not hesitate to ask God to protect us from hurt and harm.

HOW TO PRAY THE PRAYER OF JABEZ

1. Look at the specific ways God has blessed your life. Thank him. Ask him to continue to bless you.

2. Consider new areas for your own ministry—ways to "enlarge your border." What talents do you have that could be used in God's service? Talk with God about this. Listen for his prompting. Ask him to identify new opportunities.

3. Think about times that God's hand has helped you in the last year, even in the last week. Ask for more strength and guidance in the future—especially if you're stepping out to grab a new opportunity for ministry.

4. Ask for God's protection from spiritual and physical harm.

THE SHEPHERD PSALM
Psalm 23

THE LORD IS my shepherd, I
shall not want.
He makes me lie down in
green pastures;
he leads me beside still waters,
he restores my soul.
He leads me in right paths for his
name's sake.
Even though I walk through the
darkest valley, I fear no evil;
for you are with me;
your rod and your staff—they
comfort me.
You prepare a table before me in the
presence of my enemies;
you anoint my head with oil;
my cup overflows.
Surely goodness and mercy shall
follow me
all the days of my life,
and I shall dwell in the house of the
Lord
my whole life long.

Delighting in God's Protection

THE BIBLE HAS more than 500 references to sheep or shepherds. In ancient Israel, herding was a common trade. Of course, the biblical writers often used it as a metaphor for our relationship with God. Nowadays, we might say *the Lord is my accountant* or *the Lord is my construction worker*, and we'd develop whole analogies based on those trades. But there's a beauty in the ancient image of the shepherd. So let's go back to a different time and enter David's world of sheep and shepherds.

If we were to pray Psalm 23 truthfully, we might have to say, "*When* the Lord is my shepherd, I do not want." In our world, there are many sheep in shepherd's clothing, and

they bombard us with all-too-perfect promises of unnaturally green pastures and eerily quiet waters. Yet, when we follow them, we soon discover it's all a mirage. We're left standing in a desert, weary from hunger and thirst. The question is: Who are we following, and why?

Look around you and you'll see a herd of shepherds calling for your attention. What would happen if you completed the following sentences honestly?

"When *I* am my shepherd..."
"When *money* is my shepherd..."
"When *my friends* are my shepherd..."

It's obvious that none of these can lead to the satisfaction found in the green pastures God has set aside for us. They can't satisfy our ultimate hunger or quench the thirst of our souls. Only when the Lord is our shepherd do we feel satisfied with who we are and what we have.

"Life is a journey," proclaims one recent TV commercial. The psalmist would agree. We are being led *to* green pastures, *beside* still waters, and *through* the darkest valley. We might try this journey on our own, afraid to follow God or ask directions, but ultimately we'll get lost and end up in a ditch somewhere. Elsewhere, the Bible says, "All we like sheep have gone astray; we have all turned to our own way" (Isaiah 53:6). But Jesus tells of a shepherd who leaves the flock safe in its fold to hunt for one stray lamb—and he rejoices when he finds it. In case anyone missed the point, Jesus explained that the stray lamb is the sinner who repents, causing great joy in heaven (Luke 15:3-7). Psalm 23 helps us to hear the shepherd's voice and return to him.

Dark valleys can confuse us. We go through periods of suffering and doubt when we're not sure where the shepherd is or whether he still cares about us. And we don't know what dangers are lurking in the shadows. But this psalm communicates a faith that works even in the dark. If the shepherd has been leading us through the idyllic pastures without fail, why would he abandon us in the danger zones? He wouldn't, of course! He is with us, so what do we have to be afraid of?

David, the shepherd-king credited with writing this psalm, once boasted about killing a lion and a bear that were threatening his sheep. This psalm certainly doesn't deny the existence of evil forces; it just knows that we have a shepherd who can wrestle them into submission. As we pray in the Lord's Prayer, "Deliver us from evil." It's a dangerous world, and some valleys are darker than others, but the Lord has the power to protect us. Note also that we walk *through* the darkest valley—which means that God will lead us out of it. The outcome of trying times may not be what we expect, but God promises to be with us from start to finish.

In the second part of this psalm, it's time to celebrate. The Lord leads us to safety and then throws a banquet for us. All those enemies who tried to pull us down are there at the party, but we are the guests of honor. Anointing with oil was a ritual of cleansing and refreshing, something like the hot towel they give first-class passengers at the end of a long flight. And our cup overflows with a satisfying beverage.

Now we see the Lord in a new light. As our shepherd, he has used rod and staff to guide us through the ups and downs of life. He has shown himself to be strong and wise, comforting and protecting, nourishing and sustaining. But now at the banquet he is our gracious host, blessing and forgiving, humble and attentive, joyful and generous. Amazingly, *he* is serving *us,* refreshing us with oil, keeping our cup full. Jesus once said that he did not come "to be served, but to serve" (Mark 10:45). That's what we see here.

This psalm begins with a picture of the Lord leading us. It ends with his great love following us. God's goodness and mercy attend us wherever we go. They may not always be evident, but they are always there. When we allow him to be our Shepherd, that's the story of our lives.

HOW TO PRAY THE SHEPHERD PSALM

Take this psalm line by line, inserting yourself into it and praying it to the Lord.

1. *You are my shepherd, Lord, I shall not want.*

Think about all the longings that the Lord fulfills.

2. *You make me lie down in green pastures; you lead me beside still waters, you restore my soul.*

Where has God led you lately? Have you allowed yourself to follow him? How has he refreshed you?

3. *You lead me in right paths for your name's sake.*

How has God helped you to make the right choices?

4. *Even though I walk through the darkest valley, I fear no evil; for you are with me; your rod and your staff—they comfort me.*

Be specific about dark times you've gone through. Thank the Lord for getting you through them.

5. *You prepare a table before me in the presence of my enemies; you anoint my head with oil; my cup overflows.*

Thank him for the special times you have with him, both the worship services and the private times. Thank him for all the joy he brings you.

6. *Surely goodness and mercy shall follow me all the days of my life, and I shall dwell in your house my whole life long.*

Consider what your relationship with God will be like five, ten, even twenty years from now.

THE LORD'S PRAYER
Matthew 6:9–13

OUR FATHER in heaven,
hallowed be your name.
Your kingdom come.
Your will be done,
on earth as it is in heaven.
Give us this day our daily bread.
And forgive us our debts,
as we also have forgiven our debtors.
And do not bring us to the time of
trial,
but rescue us from the evil one.

LEARNING TO PRAY

THERE'S SOMETHING ironic about reciting the Lord's Prayer. Millions of Christians have used this model in their own quiet times with God. Many churches recite it each week. Countless believers turn to it in times of need. Most Christians learn it early in life or soon after they commit to Christ. Soon they can speak the words from memory, without even thinking about them.

Without even thinking about them. There's the irony. Just a few moments before he gave his followers this prayer, Jesus cautioned them to avoid the errors of "the Gentiles" who "heap up empty phrases" because "they think that they will be heard because of their many words" (Matthew 6:7). All too often we have turned the Lord's Prayer into exactly that: empty phrases (the King James Version uses the term "vain repetitions"). We begin to treat this prayer like magic words that will get us what we want. That's certainly not what Jesus intended.

This prayer is an outline for the various types of conversation we have with God. It's a skeleton that we "flesh out" with the details of our lives and longings. It's the frame upon which we construct our prayer life.

Does that mean we should never recite the Lord's Prayer? Not at all. It provides an ideal meeting ground for public prayer. When any group of believers prays together, they need a common text. Ideally, each person would silently fill in the personal details of the "daily bread" they need or the temptation they face. And there are also moments when we as individuals don't know what to pray. We feel distant from God or unsure of what to say. In such uncertain times, you can't go wrong with the Lord's own prayer. These words can prime the pump of faith and get you back on speaking terms with your Father in heaven.

From Relationship to Rescue

JESUS' PRAYER begins with **relationship**. Other Jewish prayers of the time hailed God as the King of the Universe, the Creator of all, and that's very appropriate. Yes, he is that, but the revolutionary teaching of Jesus was that God wants a relationship with us, like that of a parent with a child.

The world is full of people who do not completely understand the words they grew up praying. One example of this is *hallowed,* and it simply means **holy**. As we read the Old Testament, we see people and things becoming "holy" as they connect with God. Holiness seems to be godliness, and it goes without saying that God is godly. But we get a clue from the English language: *holy* is related to the word *whole*. When we come in contact with God, he makes us whole, complete. He is the essence of wholeness, and we find our wholeness in him. So don't get scared away by the idea of God being "hallowed" or holy. It just means that he has what you're lacking.

Jesus spent a lot of time preaching about God's **kingdom**. He told stories about it that challenged people's assumptions. The kingdom of God is like a tiny mustard seed that grows into a huge tree. It's like a merchant who invests his whole fortune in one pearl. It's like a party where the A-list doesn't show up, so the host invites beggars from the street. People were anticipating a future time when God would set up his kingdom on earth, reigning from Jerusalem over all the nations. Jesus kept saying that God's kingdom wasn't just a "there and then," it was also a "here and now." God's kingdom is wherever and whenever people honor him as their king. When we pray for his kingdom to come, we are raising his flag *now* in our hearts.

Some people are confused by the phrase "your **will** be done." Doesn't God do what he wants anyway? Maybe so, but as we pray this, we are communicating our compliance. We are saying, "We want what you want, Lord." It's not just a vague wish, it's a commitment to live the way he wants us to live.

As the Israelites wandered the desert in Moses' day, they knew all about **daily bread**. God sent manna from heaven each day to sustain them. But if someone tried to hoard any manna, it quickly spoiled. They had to trust God to provide for them each day. Nowadays, if you're thoroughly insured, well capitalized, and securely invested, you might miss out on the joy of God's daily provision, but there are still needs that occur. Jesus says we should ask God for what we need.

Confession is also part of this model prayer, but there's a catch. We ask God to forgive our **debts** (or trespasses), but we are expected to offer forgiveness to others. Jesus told a story about a servant who was forgiven a million-dollar debt but then demanded payment of a few dollars from someone else. That's not the way it's supposed to work. Forgiven people are expected to forgive others. It's not just a transaction, it's a change of heart. Once you understand how much God has forgiven you, your heart melts in mercy toward others.

This prayer concludes with a plea for deliverance from **temptation** (or "the time of trial") and from **evil** (that is, the devil). There are two stages of protection requested: We don't want to face trials, but if we do, we don't want the evil one to triumph over us. The first request is sometimes denied. Believers will face trials. Just two chapters earlier, we find Jesus being led into temptation by the Spirit (Matthew 4:1), and yet he was given strength against the evil one. There is no shame in praying to avoid difficult times, but we must recognize that often God uses them to help us grow. In the Garden of Gethsemane, Jesus prayed that the time of trial would be removed. It wasn't. But then he invoked another part of the Lord's Prayer when he said, "Your will be done" (Mark 14:36). When we do face trials, we can be assured that God will deliver us from evil.

How to Pray the Lord's Prayer

Take the time to go through the Lord's Prayer line by line, filling in the details of your life.

1. *Our Father in heaven . . .*

Think about your relationship with God. Bask in his love.

2. *. . . hallowed be your name.*

What are you lacking in life? Consider how God can make you whole.

3. *Your kingdom come. Your will be done, on earth as it is in heaven.*

Honor God as your king, and consider what he might want you to do. How do your wants compare with his plans?

4. *Give us this day our daily bread.*

What needs do you have today? Bring them before the Lord.

5. *And forgive us our debts, as we also have forgiven our debtors.*

Confess your sins before God. Accept the forgiveness he offers through Christ. Think about other relationships in which you might need to offer or request forgiveness.

6. *And do not bring us to the time of trial, but rescue us from the evil one.*

What temptations and trials are you facing? Talk with God about them. Ask him for strength when temptation is toughest.

CHAPTER TWO

PRAYERS
for HELP

SONG FOR A SON
1 Samuel 2:1–10

HANNAH PRAYED and said, "My heart exults in the Lord; my strength is exalted in my God. My mouth derides my enemies, because I rejoice in my victory. There is no Holy One like the Lord, no one besides you; there is no Rock like our God. Talk no more so very proudly, let not arrogance come from your mouth; for the Lord is a God of knowledge, and by him actions are weighed. The bows of the mighty are broken, but the feeble gird on strength. Those who

were full have hired themselves out
for bread, but those who were hungry are fat with spoil. The barren
has borne seven, but she who has
many children is forlorn. The Lord
kills and brings to life; he brings
down to Sheol and raises up. The
Lord makes poor and makes rich; he
brings low, he also exalts. He raises
up the poor from the dust; he lifts
the needy from the ash heap, to make
them sit with princes and inherit a
seat of honor. For the pillars of the
earth are the Lord's, and on them he
has set the world. He will guard the
feet of his faithful ones, but the
wicked shall be cut off in darkness;
for not by might does one prevail.
The Lord! His adversaries shall be
shattered; the Most High will thunder in heaven. The Lord will judge
the ends of the earth; he will give
strength to his king, and exalt the
power of his anointed."

Overcoming Obstacles Through Prayer

HER BIOLOGICAL clock was ticking, and Hannah wanted a child. Her husband, Elkanah, was not rushing her; he was happy just to have her as his wife. Also, his other wife, Peninnah, had children already, and he was not in a hurry to have more. But Hannah was. Peninnah constantly teased her about her inability to conceive, often provoking Hannah to tears.

So one day when Hannah "was deeply distressed...and wept bitterly," she made a vow. If God would give her a son, she would give that son back to God. She would allow him to be raised as a Nazirite, someone specially dedicated to God. She would give him to the priest to raise, letting the boy grow up in the tabernacle.

The priest, Eli, saw Hannah praying silently, and at first he thought she must be drunk. Her lips moved, but no sound was made. She replied that she was deeply troubled. "I have been pouring out my soul before the Lord" (1 Samuel 1:15). The priest blessed her, adding his prayer that her prayer would be answered.

It was. She gave birth to a son and named him Samuel. When the boy was about three years old, she brought him to the tabernacle and presented him to Eli, saying, "I am the woman who was standing here in your presence, praying to the Lord. For this child I prayed; and the Lord has granted me the petition that I made to him. Therefore I have lent him to the Lord" (1 Samuel 1:26–28). And then Hannah offered her prayer-song of praise.

THE JOY OF ANSWERED PRAYER

HANNAH'S PRAYER is one of genuine joy and adoration for God because he listens to those who pray to him, and he helps those who admit their need for him. How often do we ask God to deliver us from a situation and then fail to give him thanks and praise when our request is granted? Almost four years after God answered her prayer to conceive, Hannah was still uttering thanks.

At first glance, Hannah's prayer-song might seem out of place. It's a social commentary. She's talking about "victory" and "enemies" and God breaking the "bows of the mighty." David the soldier might have written something like this, but Hannah? Yet we should consider her situation. Barrenness was a disgrace for women in her culture. She prayed for God to conquer it, and he did. She was even teased by a woman who was "rich" with children. By turning to the Lord, Hannah saw herself exalted into the state of motherhood.

The beauty of this song is that it shows God working in everyday life. If you read Joshua and Judges, you might get the idea that God

only cares about warfare. He helps generals, armies, and nations. But Hannah teaches us that God also grants victory to a woman who wants a baby. He is continually exalting the poor, challenging the rich, and guarding the feet of the faithful—not just in the front page news of nations and armies, but in the day-to-day existence of families as well.

Hannah's prayer is very similar to another song of exaltation, Mary's *Magnificat* (Luke 1:46–55). Both use the occasion of mother-hood to sing about the wonderful ways that God works. Both talk about how God brings down kings and lifts the lowly. And in both cases, God brings a special person into the world: Jesus and Samuel. The role of Jesus in achieving God's purposes is obvious. But Samuel, Hannah's son, also played a pivotal role in Israel's history. He brought order to chaos at the time of the judges. When King Saul became too proud, Samuel announced that the throne would be taken away. And Samuel found the new king tending sheep in Bethlehem: a lowly herder named David. So Hannah's prayer also hints at the kind of life her son would have.

There's an old Sunday school saying: "You're never too little to be used by God, but he can't use you if you're too big." Hannah's song captures that simple truth. She acknowledges "not by might does one prevail" (1 Samuel 2:9), but when we depend on God, we thrive. In her weakness, Hannah was able to admit her dependence on God. In our self-reliant, do-it-yourself, individualistic world, it can be hard to admit that we need God. But a child who does not depend on a parent will soon grow hungry and seek food; in the same way, we grow weak when we go it alone. God calls us to rely on him for nourishment and for strength in all that we do.

HOW TO PRAY THE PRAYER OF HANNAH

1. Be joyful. Think about the victories God has granted you.

2. Recognize the sovereignty of God and his control over all aspects of your life.

3. Bring your sincere requests before the Lord.

4. Thank him when he answers.

SHOWDOWN ON MOUNT CARMEL
1 Kings 18:36–37

THE PROPHET Elijah came near and said, "O Lord, God of Abraham, Isaac, and Israel, let it be known this day that you are God in Israel, that I am your servant, and that I have done all these things at your bidding. Answer me, O Lord, answer me, so that this people may know that you, O Lord, are God, and that you have turned their hearts back."

A Miraculous Demonstration
of God's Power

THE SCENE must have been electric. These days it would be covered live on all the networks, hyped around the clock as the day approached. The prophet Elijah, the mysterious man from the wrong side of the river, was challenging the royal prophets to a duel on Mount Carmel. Each side would prepare a bull for sacrifice upon an altar and then call their god to rain down fire from heaven to consume it.

King Ahab and Queen Jezebel had led the Israelites away from their traditional beliefs and into the worship of regional fertility gods, primarily the sky-god Baal. Elijah had spoken courageously against this, but sometimes he felt like he was the only one who did so. On Mount Carmel, it was 450 against one. "The god who answers by fire is indeed God," Elijah challenged, as he reviewed the rules of this showdown.

The Baal-worshipers started early in the morning and worked all day, readying the sacrifice and calling out to their deity. At noon, Elijah began to add some fun to the proceedings, urging them to pray louder, suggesting that Baal might be off traveling or catching a nap. Desperately, the royal prophets began to cut themselves with swords, letting their blood gush over them.

At the end of the day, Scripture records the score: Baal had supplied "no voice, no answer, and no response."

Rebuilding the broken altar, Elijah prepared the sacrifice and poured water over the entire altar, filling a trench he had dug around it. There would be no room for questions about this miracle. Then he prayed this prayer.

The Bible says, "Then the fire of the Lord fell and consumed the burnt offering, the wood, the stones, and the dust, and even licked up the water that was in the trench." Public opinion immediately swayed back to Elijah's God. The prayer had been answered.

SHORT AND STEEP

A FTER HIS opponents called on their god all day, Elijah spoke two simple sentences. Sometimes people think they have to use flowery words or pious phrases, going on and on about why God should answer their prayers. But all those words become babble to God. Jesus chided the Gentiles who thought God would hear them because they talked a lot (Matthew 6:7). God much prefers the plain, honest words of our hearts. As Proverbs 17:27–28 says, "One who spares words is knowledgeable."

Notice also how Elijah raised the stakes in this encounter. By pouring water on the sacrifice, he made it even harder for fire to consume it. But he knew who he was dealing with. God wouldn't blink an eye at that challenge. Elijah had complete confidence in God's power.

This doesn't mean that we should randomly demand outrageous miracles from God. Many kids (and even a few adults) have tested Jesus' teachings about faith moving mountains by ordering Mount Everest to relocate to Australia. That misses the point. We need to be so in touch with God that we know which mountains he wants to move. That's what faith is all about. And that's exactly

what Elijah had. Who do you think sent him to Mount Carmel to begin with?

The prayer itself is inspiring. Elijah invokes the God of the patriarchs, using Jacob's alternate name, Israel, because it was also the name of the nation Elijah was summoning back to God. He wants the Lord to demonstrate two things: God's power and the validity of Elijah's ministry. That might seem self-serving, but Elijah was playing a key role in this drama. Many Israelites probably knew the Lord as "Elijah's God." In fact, Elijah's name means "The Lord (Jah, God's personal name) is my God (Eli)."

In the same way, we might find ourselves representing God in front of certain neighbors and friends. We won't be offering bulls on altars in the backyard, but we might speak up for the Lord in various ways. Our culture worships things such as money, pleasure, beauty, and sports. When God asks us to challenge those idols, we can surely ask him for support.

Yet the ultimate goal of Elijah's prayer was not personal pride but the return of Israel to God. As Jesus told a Samaritan woman, God seeks people to worship him (John 4:23). You can't read very far in Scripture without hearing this message loud and clear. He still seeks worshipers today. We can confidently pray that God would turn people's hearts to him.

HOW TO PRAY THE PRAYER OF ELIJAH

1. Think through the names of people in your life. Are there some who need to turn to God? Ask God about this.

2. In your prayer time, consider ways that God might show one of these people that he really is God. Try to see God's priorities.

3. Pray that God would "prove himself" to this person. Use the prayer of Elijah, adapting it to the specific details. Then ask if God wants you to help out in some way.

MY BROTHER'S KEEPER
Genesis 32:9–12

O GOD OF MY father Abraham and God of my father Isaac, O Lord who said to me, "Return to your country and to your kindred, and I will do you good," I am not worthy of the least of all the steadfast love and all the faithfulness that you have shown to your servant, for with only my staff I crossed this Jordan; and now I have become two companies. Deliver me, please, from the hand of my brother, from the hand of Esau, for I am afraid of him; he may come and kill us all, the mothers with the children. Yet you have said, "I will surely do you good, and make your offspring as the sand of the sea, which cannot be counted because of their number."

Praying for Deliverance

TALK ABOUT dysfunctional families! First, Jacob cheated his older brother, Esau, out of the family inheritance. Then, with the help of his mother, he disguised himself as Esau and received the sacred blessing from their blind and dying father. When Esau discovered what Jacob had done, he vowed to kill him as soon as their father died. Hearing of this plan, Jacob fled and successfully avoided Esau for 20 years.

During that time, Jacob had a few new adventures, such as getting married—twice—and fathering a caravan of kids. But his father-in-law was just as much of a trickster as he was, so Jacob eventually decided to move back to his homeland. By this time he was a wealthy man, with flocks and herds and servants (and, of course, all those children). But along the journey he received word that Esau was coming to meet him with an army of 400 men. This made Jacob more than a little nervous.

He didn't have a lot of time. Jacob quickly split his possessions and his family into two

traveling parties so that if one group was attacked, the other could escape. Then he launched his frantic and desperate plea for God's protection.

The prayer is both comical and touching. Jacob begins by reminding God that he is only in this predicament because he followed God's will—as if to say, "You're the one who got me into this mess, and you told me that everything would be fine if I listened to you." That's Jacob, always seeking an upper hand in negotiations.

But then Jacob offers thanks to God for the blessings he has received at his hand. There is a sense of genuine gratitude and adoration as Jacob explains that he had nothing when he crossed the Jordan River, and now everything that he has he owes to God. He knows in his heart that God is in control, but his head can't stop worrying about his angry brother approaching with that battalion.

HONEST AND FAITHFUL

JACOB IS hardly a paragon of virtue. As we read the stories in Genesis about him, he often appears selfish, dishonest, and mischievous. And still there is a lot we can learn from him. Most of all, he keeps in touch with God. This is the man who wrestled with God one night in a dream. That could be a picture of Jacob's entire life. He didn't always make the right moves, but he never let go of God. For imperfect folks like us, that's a pretty good lesson to learn.

And this prayer gives us an interesting combination of honesty and fragile faith. Sometimes we sacrifice honesty for faith. For example, Jacob could have acted as if he was not scared of his advancing brother. He could have said, "God, I know that everything will be all right. I have complete faith in you." But that wouldn't have been honest. Instead, Jacob is both honest and faithful, admitting "I am afraid of [Esau]," but still clinging to

God's promise to do good for him. Jacob is truly scared, but that does not mean that he thinks God will let him down. When we pray about a situation—whether it's financial, work-related, or involving a relationship—we should be honest with God about our fears and look honestly at the possible outcomes. But we should also trust that God will get us through the situation, often with better results than we could have imagined.

That's what happened to Jacob. When they finally met, Esau ran and hugged him. It was a time of rejoicing. God did keep his promises, as he always does.

HOW TO PRAY THE PRAYER OF JACOB

1. In a crisis, don't forget God's previous blessings and promises.

2. Don't be afraid to be honest about your feelings. God knows them anyway. There's no point in pretending to be stronger than you are. Give your doubts to God, and he will bolster your faith.

3. Feel free to remind God of his promises, as many people in Scripture have done. But trust God to find amazing new ways to fulfill those promises.

THY WILL BE DONE

Mark 14:36

H E SAID, "Abba, Father, for you all things are possible; remove this cup from me; yet, not what I want, but what you want."

NOT MY WILL . . .

I T WAS the last night before the crucifixion. Jesus enjoyed the Passover meal with his disciples and then took them to a secluded place on the Mount of Olives, the Garden of Gethsemane. The gospel of Mark says that Jesus "began to be distressed and agitated." He left his disciples, urging them to stay awake and went off by himself to pray.

Jesus had plenty to be distressed and agitated about. In the three years of his ministry, he had made enemies among the religious elite. Though he had been warned not to make this Passover trip to Jerusalem, he insisted. He had told his disciples that a cross awaited him, and yet he had entered the city to triumphal shouts. He had faced off against the moneychangers in the temple, and in those last days he had continued his public teaching.

It seemed that as long as he was in public the authorities wouldn't arrest him, fearing a reaction by the people. They needed to find him alone, or with only his disciples, so they could take him without causing a scene. But Jesus dodged them effectively for a few days. That's why they needed Judas to lead the way to him. Even in planning the site of the Last Supper, Jesus employed secrecy, telling some disciples to meet a mysterious man carrying water and to follow him home. Perhaps that was so Judas wouldn't know in advance where they'd be dining. Jesus wanted those last precious hours with his friends.

Finally, he was in the garden, begging his disciples to stay awake—probably for their own protection. He might have already seen the train of torches snaking through the valley and up the mountain—Judas leading the temple guard to arrest him. Distressed and agitated? You would have been, too.

A Deep Intimacy

IN THIS time of crisis, he turned to his Father in prayer. "Abba, Father," he began, and already we get a sense of their relationship. *Abba* is an Aramaic word used by children. The best English translation is something like "Daddy." There was a deep intimacy between Father and Son.

We take for granted the idea of God as Father, but actually it seldom appears in the Old Testament. The psalmist likens God to a father who cares for his children (Psalm 103:13), and has God calling the Israelite king (and the coming Messiah) his Son (Psalm 2:7). But Jesus was one step ahead when he invited his followers to address God as "our Father" and in his repeated references to "the Father in heaven." Yet the word *Abba* makes it clear that he's not just talking about "Our Father" but "*my* Father." More accurately, he means "my Daddy." Whatever else he prays in this situation, it's based on this tight-knit relationship.

To use a trivial comparison, consider the teenager who asks for the car keys. "Daddy,

you're the best!" Sure, that might be some phony buttering up, but at least the child knows that the request is built on the relationship. No stranger is going to hand over the keys, but Daddy might.

Jesus continues his prayer in much the same way: *Abba*, you're the best. All things are possible for you. God can do anything. Amazingly, Jesus was suggesting that there might be some other way to fulfill God's plan, a way that wouldn't involve his cruel crucifixion. At least he was hoping there might be.

In our lives, we often get distressed and agitated by matters that are beyond our

control. It helps to realize that God is not locked into our limitations. We assume there are, maybe, two or three possible outcomes, each equally bad. But God has the power to do a million amazing things beyond what we ask or even think. As we pray, we should acknowledge his limitation-breaking ability.

In the garden, Jesus went on to ask for what he wanted. Could he get through this without having to drink the cup of suffering? Obviously, he knew there was great pain ahead—physical and spiritual. Who can blame him for wanting to avoid it, if possible?

Ultimately, Jesus offered his submission. After presenting his own "will"—what he wanted to happen—he bowed to his Father's will. As

Matthew records it (and in the venerable King James Version), "Thy will be done." Our own desires take shape only as they conform to God's desires.

How to Pray the "Thy Will Be Done" Prayer

1. Bask in your relationship with the Lord. All your requests and God's responses will be based on this relationship. And when you're distressed and agitated, it helps to fall into the arms of the one who loves you most.

2. Let God open your eyes to new possibilities. All things are possible with God. He might have a way out of your mess that you haven't thought of. Acknowledge his power to get things done.

3. Tell God what you want. Some people are afraid of this, but it's just being honest. "If I were in your place, Lord, this is what I'd do." Jesus instructed his disciples to ask God to meet their needs.

4. Give in to God's desires. "Of course I'm not in your place, Lord. You're the boss. You have a better idea." After sharing the possibilities and your desires, ask God to follow through on the situation with his own perfect wisdom.

CHAPTER THREE

PRAYERS for GROWTH

A WISH FOR WISDOM
1 Kings 3:6–9

YOU HAVE shown great and steadfast love to your servant, my father David, because he walked before you in faithfulness, in righteousness, and in uprightness of heart toward you; and you have kept for him this great and steadfast love, and have given him a son to sit on his throne today. And now, O Lord my God, you have made your servant king in place of my father David, although I am only a little child; I do not know how to go out or come in. And your servant is in the midst of the people whom you have chosen, a great people, so numerous they cannot be numbered or counted. Give your servant therefore an understanding mind to govern your people, able to discern between good and evil; for who can govern this your great people?

ASKING GOD FOR WISDOM

FOR MOST of its history, Israel was a nation in the middle. After their miraculous escape from slavery in Egypt and a 40-year hiatus in the desert, the Israelites settled into their land. But they had to fight for every acre, displacing various Canaanite groups. And then the coastal Philistines moved inland every so often to grab more territory. Later in Israel's history, they were squeezed between the superpowers of Egypt and Assyria, Babylon, and Persia. But for one brief, shining period in the 900s B.C., Israel was the richest and strongest country in the Mideast. The king at the time was Solomon.

He was the third king of Israel. During the settlement period, a motley collection of regional judges held power. The prophet Samuel, a judge himself, did much to unite the various tribes, but the people wanted a king. So Samuel selected a tall but brooding warrior named Saul. He was a disaster. In jealousy, he turned the nation's military resources against his best soldier, David. When Saul died in battle against the

Philistines, David assumed the throne, restoring order to the monarchy. He built Israel's military presence, neutralizing the Philistines and other foes, and he made plans to build a great temple for the Lord.

When David died, his son Solomon picked up where he left off, building the Temple and other ornate structures as well as improving the economy. Solomon was brilliant at international relations, establishing trade with partners throughout the Mediterranean, Asia, and Africa. Israel was geographically the center of the known world, and it used that position to fill its coffers.

But Solomon also became famous for his wisdom. People came from far and wide to meet with him and talk to him. Where did he get such wisdom? That's where this prayer comes in.

Solomon had been king for a short time when the Lord appeared to him in a dream, offering him anything he wanted. "Ask what I should give you," the Lord said. What would you ask for? Wealth? Pleasure? Power? Solomon asked for "an understanding mind." Offered anything in the world, he wanted wisdom— and the rest is history.

THE WISDOM OF SOLOMON

SOLOMON ALREADY showed some wisdom in praying his prayer. Here's where we see it.

First, **he knew who he was.** Yes, he was the son of the great King David, but he didn't assume that made him a worthy successor. He considered himself "a little child." Faced with the huge task of ruling God's people, he didn't know his way around. Many of us feel unworthy when we begin a new job or begin to explore new territory. That's good. We can only grow when we realize that we need to grow. Solomon knew the awesome challenge that lay before him. He had big sandals to fill, and he knew he needed help. That's one mark of true wisdom.

Solomon also knew **where to find true power**. Notice how he used the term "your servant" four times in this prayer. He knew who the real boss was. He admitted to God that those he governed were "your people." Other kings would boast about ruling "my people," but Solomon knew better. He gave God credit for helping his father, and he understood that he, Solomon, would need a lot more help. He would find it in God's "great and steadfast love."

Ultimately, Solomon knew **what had true value**. In one variation of an age-old tale, a genie offers a man three wishes. He asks for money and gets it. He asks for power and

gets it. Then he asks for more wishes. In a way, that third wish is Solomon's. He knew that the wealth and power he already had would be worthless without the wisdom to use them properly. Implied in this request is the idea that Solomon would understand what God wanted. He wanted to "discern between good and evil"; he wanted to know God's way. In our prayers, we often ask God to agree with our plans when we should be asking for the wisdom to discern his plans. Solomon knew the greatest gift he could ask for was the wisdom to know what was right. That's a gift we should prize as well.

How to Pray the Prayer of Solomon

1. Tell God who you are: a child, needing to grow. You don't have the wisdom you need, and you know it.

2. Tell God how great he is. Name the great things you have seen him do, both in your life and in the lives of those around you. Acknowledge that you need his power.

3. Ask God for an understanding mind, a discerning heart, and the wisdom to know right from wrong. Ask him to teach you his ways.

ROOTED AND GROUNDED
Ephesians 3:16–21

I PRAY THAT, according to the riches of his glory, he may grant that you may be strengthened in your inner being with power through his Spirit, and that Christ may dwell in your hearts through faith, as you are being rooted and grounded in love. I pray that you may have the power to comprehend, with all the saints, what is the breadth and length and height and depth, and to know the love of Christ that surpasses knowledge, so that you may be filled with all the fullness of God. Now to him who by the power at work within us is able to accomplish abundantly far more than all we can ask or imagine, to him be glory in the church and in Christ Jesus to all generations, forever and ever. Amen.

Inner Strength

IN THIS PRAYER, Paul lists several things that he's praying for, and the first two go together. He wants his readers to be "strengthened in your inner being," and he wants Christ to "dwell in your hearts." These are two ways of saying the same thing.

If you've been to a gym lately, you've seen people working on strengthening their *outer* beings. Many are committed to pumping up, slimming down, and toning their muscles so their bodies have a stronger-looking outer appearance. Paul wants that sort of attention focused on the *inner* being.

But who's doing the work here? The Spirit is supplying the power. This seems to be a natural result of Christ taking up residence in our hearts. Perhaps it's like inviting Arnold Schwarzenegger to move into your home; before you know it, he'll have you pumping iron like a champ. Except we're talking about *inner* fitness, and Christ is our heart-guest. He affects us in deeply personal ways and empowers us with his Spirit.

It's interesting that Paul doesn't give many details about how this strengthening occurs. This is a prayer, after all, not a do-it-yourself manual. The only hint we get is one phrase at the end of verse 17, and it's a beauty.

The process of inner strength involves "being rooted and grounded in love." *Rooted* is an agricultural term and *grounded* is architectural. First-century Ephesus was a town in transition. As with many American cities, there was farmland all around the area, but then a building boom attracted people to the urban area. The citizens knew about the importance of good roots, which draw up nutrients from the soil. They were learning about the importance of a good foundation. At the end of chapter 2, Paul describes the church as "built upon the foundation of the apostles and prophets, with Christ Jesus himself as the cornerstone. In him the whole structure is joined together and grows into a holy temple to the Lord; in whom you also are built together spiritually into a dwelling place for God" (Ephesians 2:20–22). There, too, he seems to mix metaphors of farming and building. The process of Christian growth combines both of those things as well. We all need good grounding.

And love is what we sink our roots into. It's what we build upon. It is the starting point of our inner lives.

COMPREHEND?

THE SECOND thing Paul prays is that the people would comprehend "what is the breadth and length and height and depth..." Of what? Even in the original Greek, this thought is stopped midsentence. But if you look at the phrases before and after this verse it will be clear to see that he is talking about love.

When New York City's Empire State Building was constructed, it was the tallest building on Earth. People marveled at its size, barely comprehending how a building could be that tall. That's the image Paul has of God's love. He wants people not only to "get it" but to *grasp* it. He wants them to put their arms around the hugeness of Christ's love. Yes, it surpasses knowledge, he says, but as Christ moves into their hearts they can make this love a part of their lives.

There was a group known as the Gnostics that became quite prominent in the second century, but we have hints that their ideas were brewing back in Paul's time. Taking

some pieces of Christianity, they merged them with parts of Greek philosophy to develop an elaborate system of beliefs. These teachers claimed to have a secret knowledge (*gnosis* in Greek) that few possessed. Others might know little bits and pieces of God, but these privileged "knowers" knew God in his fullness. Or so they said.

We have various groups like that around today, peddling their secret paths to the fullness of God. Paul was clearly launching a barrage against these teachers when he talked about the love of Christ surpassing *gnosis*. Grounded in this love, and not in any secret "knowledge," these Ephesians could experience God's fullness.

Ask and Imagine

PAUL'S BENEDICTION is powerful. You might expect him to assure us that God has the power to give us what we ask for. No, God can do far more than that, more than we could even imagine. What's more, that power is *at work within us*.

Many philosophies, like that of the Gnostics of old and their modern counterparts, have thrived on making people feel weak and inadequate. Sadly, some Christian teachers have done the same. Sure, we are weak without Christ's power, but that's a moot point once Christ is living in our hearts. Now we have an amazing power working inside of us. If we stay grounded in the incomprehensible love of Christ, the Spirit can do things in us, through us, and around us that are beyond our wildest dreams.

How to Pray the "Rooted and Grounded" Prayer

1. If you don't know that Christ is dwelling in your heart, invite him to do so.

2. Ask Christ to strengthen your inner being.

3. Meditate on the amazing love of Christ.

4. Ask God what powerful thing he wants to do through you.

5. Pray Ephesians 3:16–21 for someone else.

AN APOSTLE'S PRAYER
Philippians 1:9–11

ND THIS IS my prayer, that your love may overflow more and more with knowledge and full insight, to help you determine what is best, so that in the day of Christ you may be pure and blameless, having produced the harvest of righteousness that comes through Jesus Christ for the glory and praise of God.

GROWING IN LOVE AND INSIGHT

PAUL WROTE this letter from prison, either in Rome or Ephesus, yet it is filled with joy. He had been jailed for preaching the message of Christ, but he doesn't bemoan his own situation. Instead he finds the good in it—he was actually spreading the gospel among the soldiers who guarded him! It's clear that he deeply appreciates the Philippians, who have supported him with prayers and gifts. And so, as he begins most of his letters, he offers thanks to his readers and then prays for them.

Imagine the things he could have prayed. "This is my prayer: that many more people would join the Philippian church...that they would be strong as they face discrimination and persecution for the sake of Christ...that life would go well for the members there, free of illness or tragedy...that I'll be able to get out of jail!" Any of those would be fine things to pray for, but that's not what Paul chose. Instead, he prayed for their present love to grow and deepen in knowledge and insight.

There is something foundational about this prayer and yet something quite advanced. It's as if the Philippians are entering first grade and receiving their doctorates at the same time. When Jesus was asked to name the greatest commandments in God's law, he mentioned two—love the Lord your God and love your neighbor. Love is square one. Elsewhere, Paul says that without love all the pious acts a person can do are worthless. So it shouldn't surprise us that the apostle prays for the Philippians to have love. It's pretty basic.

But what does he pray about this love? That it would overflow in "knowledge and full insight." Love isn't usually teamed with such qualities, is it? People say that love is blind, and they have a point. Your googly-eyed reaction to that special someone you see across a crowded room—well, that's hardly "knowledge and full insight." But Paul knows that true love doesn't come at first sight; it takes a lifetime of commitment. The best picture of love isn't the glazed look of the prom couple, but the people who have been married for 30 years—each one knows all the dirt about the other, and they're still committed.

Some parents show love to their children by giving them everything they want. Others know better. Insightful parents recognize that it is often better to say no. True love does what is best, even if the child doesn't like it.

The Beatles sang, "All you need is love," and who can argue with that? Love is our primary calling. But love without knowledge is naïve and vulnerable. People might think they're living in love because they try not to hurt

anyone or anything. That's a fine beginning, but it's mere puppy love compared to the deeply insightful commitment that God wants from us. There are some very loving people who are not grounded enough in knowledge to be able to stand against the pressures of doubt, criticism, or false teachings. They might not be hurting anyone, but they're not actively seeking ways to help, either.

This is the graduate degree Paul prays for, the grown-up love that understands the issues and still acts in devotion to God and others.

LOVE'S SIDE EFFECTS

THE ANCIENT Greeks loved quality. They spent lots of time theorizing about what made something beautiful or excellent or true. The

Romans appreciated moral excellence, prizing the personal characteristics that made great people great. Philippi had been Alexander the Great's home, so its culture borrowed heavily from the Greek culture that Alexander loved. But by Paul's time, the city was an outpost of the Roman army, so it also reflected Roman values. Putting these cultures together, you can understand why they'd be interested in determining "what is best."

That's what an insightful love does: It seeks to find the best option in a situation, not the easiest or most painless. Love wants the best for everyone involved, and knowledge searches for the best way to make it happen.

Later in his letter, Paul urges his readers not to argue with one another "so that you may

be blameless and innocent…in the midst of a crooked and perverse generation" (2:15). Reputation was especially important in Roman culture, so the Christians in this army town would want to be especially blameless. But we can also guess that slander was beginning to tarnish the Christians in that area. The persecution of Christians wasn't going to happen for another decade or so, but discrimination was certainly going on, and Christians probably found themselves falsely blamed for all sorts of things.

But in this prayer Paul is talking about "the day of Christ"—that future time when we stand before the Lord we've been serving. Will he be happy with us? Let your love grow rich with insight, and you will make the best choices, which will ensure that you'll stand "pure and blameless" on that day.

Here's the problem with mixing love and knowledge. The choices you make might not always *seem* the most loving. Because of your insight, you'll have to engage in "tough love" from time to time. And the choices you make won't always seem like the smartest ones.

Perhaps you'll take another chance on someone who has failed you because you know they're worth it. People might judge you on either side, blaming you for being too soft or too hard. No one will really know until your choices yield results.

Paul prays that your insightful love will lead to good choices that are planted like seeds all around you. You'll stand before the Master on that day and say, "All I did was plant some seeds," but he'll point to wagonloads of righteousness coming over the horizon. Your good choices will have yielded a rich harvest.

How to Pray the Apostle's Prayer

Why not pray this prayer for someone else? Sure, you can ask God to fill you with insightful love, but it's more fulfilling to hope this for others.

1. Choose at least one and as many as five people whom you want to pray for.

2. Think about the choices they might be facing.

3. Pray the prayer, changing pronouns as necessary. Remember: You may not know "what is best" in their situations, but God will guide them.

CHAPTER FOUR

PRAYERS *of* THANKS *and* PRAISE

VICTORY SONG
Exodus 15:1-18

THEN MOSES and the Israelites sang this song to the Lord: "I will sing to the Lord, for he has triumphed gloriously; horse and rider he has thrown into the sea. The Lord is my strength and my might, and he has become my salvation, this is my God, and I will praise him, my father's God, and I will exalt him. The Lord is a warrior; the Lord is his name.

"Pharaoh's chariots and his army he cast into the sea; his picked officers were sunk in the Red Sea. The floods covered them; they went down into the depths like a stone. Your right hand, O Lord, glorious in power—your right hand, O Lord, shattered the enemy. In the greatness of your majesty you overthrew your adversaries; you sent out your fury, it consumed them like stubble. At the blast of your nostrils the waters piled up, the floods stood up in a heap; the deeps congealed in the heart of the sea. The enemy said, 'I will overtake, I will divide the spoil, my desire shall have its fill of them. I will draw my sword, my hand shall destroy them.' You blew with your wind, the sea covered them; they sank like lead in the mighty waters.

"Who is like you, O Lord, among the gods? Who is like you, majestic in holiness, awesome in splendor, doing wonders? You stretched out your right hand, the earth swallowed them.

"In your steadfast love you led the people whom you redeemed; you guided them by your strength to your holy abode. The peoples heard, they trembled; pangs seized the inhabitants of Philistia. Then the chiefs of Edom were dismayed; trembling seized the leaders of Moab; all the inhabitants of Canaan melted away. Terror and dread fell upon them; by the might of your arm they became still as a stone until your people, O Lord, passed by, until the people whom you acquired passed by. You brought them in and planted them on the mountain of your own possession, the place, O Lord, that you made your abode, the sanctuary, O Lord, that your hands have established. The Lord will reign forever and ever."

GOD'S MIRACULOUS WORKS

HOLLYWOOD HAS perfected the chase scene. According to the formula of most action films, we see the fleeing heroes and the chasers gaining on them. Then the camera cuts back and forth until the heroes find themselves up against an insurmountable obstacle. Say, a train is crossing the road in front of them. They'll be caught for sure! But then they find some miraculous way over that obstacle—maybe using a dump truck to vault over the train. The heroes are safe!

Did you know that formula was borrowed from the book of Exodus? More than 3,000 years ago, the Israelites found themselves in a similar chase scene. Moses had brought God's demands to the Pharaoh of Egypt: "Let my people go!" Pharaoh resisted until a series of plagues weakened his nation. Eventually, he released the Israelites from slavery and sent them on their way toward Canaan.

So we see a million or more Israelites beginning their journey out of Egypt. Meanwhile, Pharaoh has second thoughts: "What have we done?" (Exodus 14:5). He sends his cavalry after the fleeing former slaves. Moses and the Israelite traveling party have reached the banks of the Red Sea; they can't go any farther. Word comes from the rear guard that Egyptian troops are gaining ground. The people complain, "So you set us free just to die out here? Aren't there enough graves in Egypt?"

But Moses turns to the Lord, who tells him to stretch his arms out over the sea. Miraculously, it parts, leaving a pathway for the Israelites to tread. God has sent a dark cloud to confuse the advancing Egyptians; they're in a panic. When all the Israelites have crossed, Moses extends his arms and the sea returns to its normal depth, drowning the Egyptians who had followed there. The Israelites move on safely toward their promised land.

As you might expect, this wondrous miracle sparked a great celebration. Moses led the people in a song of praise for God's deliverance. Miriam gathered the women. "I will sing to the Lord, for he has triumphed gloriously," they sang (Exodus 15:1, 21).

The crossing of the Red Sea became the defining moment for the Lord's people. Previously, they were just a band of slaves; now they were a nation. They once seemed to have little awareness of their God; now he had proved himself. The Scriptures often refer back to this miracle as a moment when the Lord showed his great power to save.

LIKE NO OTHER

MOST PEOPLE in the ancient world believed in multiple gods. The Egyptians had many gods that specialized in certain areas of life; so did the Canaanites and Babylonians. Some gods were associated with nations. This was how others viewed the God of Israel. No one denied that he existed; they just put him in a group with the other deities. When one nation defeated another in battle, it was seen as proof that their gods were greater than the gods of the losers.

We find this "battle of the gods" idea often in Scripture. Of course, the Lord is eager to show that he is the one and only God. But often he is exalted as being better than all the others. That's what we find in this victory song.

"Who is like you?" the people ask. The answer is, of course, no one. Majestic and awesome, the Lord God of Israel is far superior to any other nation's deity.

The verb tenses in the last paragraph of the song make it seem as if this was written after the Israelites had settled in Canaan. Some scholars think that an editor might have added extra verses to the song some time later. But it also sounds like the wishful thinking of a team that has scored a big victory in its first game. All those nations lay between Egypt and a successful settlement of the Promised Land. God would have to establish dominance over all of them, and after this first mighty miracle, was there any question about what he could do?

Yet it really wasn't as easy as these verses make it sound. Because they feared the Canaanites, Israel wandered for 40 years in the desert. Edom and Moab were fairly easy foes to vanquish once the Israelites finally got there, but the Canaanites proved pesky, and the Philistines remained tough for a few centuries. So if this section is a later edition,

it glosses over the tough realities. If it's planning ahead, we can forgive a bit of over-confidence.

But this victory song isn't just a historical relic. It is full of some very rich words that affect our lives as much as they affected the Israelites. "Steadfast love" translates the Hebrew word *hesed* about as well as any English phrase can. It is love that goes over and above what's expected, a love that lasts forever. It is God's kind of love. Redeeming is a buying back. It's very appropriate in this context, because redeeming is something done for slaves whose freedom is purchased. This victory song is clearly talking about God bringing people out of slavery and leading them to the promised land. But the verse can also refer to God's dealings with any of us in any period of history. We can become enslaved in many ways—to habits, passions, or addictions. In his steadfast love, our God can set us free.

How to Pray the Prayer of Victory

1. Think about the victories that God has accomplished in your life recently. Keep these in mind as you pray.

2. Name five other "gods" worshiped by the people around you these days. (Hint: one might be money.) Tell God how he is superior to any of those other "gods." What does he do that the others can't?

3. Read verse 13, inserting your own name or the pronoun "me" where appropriate. Thank God for his guidance and ask God for continuing strength.

MAGNIFICAT
Luke 1:46–55

AND MARY SAID, "My soul magnifies the Lord, and my spirit rejoices in God my Savior, for he has looked with favor on the lowliness of his servant. Surely, from now on all generations will call me blessed; for the Mighty One has done great things for me, and holy is his name. His mercy is for those who fear him from generation to generation. He has shown strength with his arm; he has scattered the proud in the thoughts of their hearts. He has brought down the powerful from their thrones, and lifted up the lowly; he has filled the hungry with good things, and sent the rich away empty. He has helped his servant Israel, in remembrance of his mercy, according to the promise he made to our ancestors, to Abraham and to his descendants forever."

GOD'S GREAT POWER

SHE WAS just a teenager, promised in marriage to a carpenter named Joseph. One day her life changed more than anyone could imagine. The angel Gabriel appeared to her and announced that she would bear a special child. Her son would reign over an eternal kingdom, taking the throne of David to new levels. He would be the Son of the Most High God.

Mary was stunned. First of all, she was a virgin. But the angel explained that such a miraculous birth would be possible for God. Mary responded in agreeable trust. "Here am I, the servant of the Lord; let it be with me according to your word" (Luke 1:38).

Shortly afterward, she visited with her cousin Elizabeth, who was carrying a miraculous child of her own, the child who would be known as John the Baptist. Elizabeth was full of praise for Mary, but Mary was quick to deflect it toward God. The song she sang at that point has been dubbed "The Magnificat" (from the Latin). It's a unique prayer of praise for God's actions in history, culminating in his gift of the Christ-child to a poor Jewish girl.

MARY'S MAGNIFYING GLASS

ARY BEGINS her song by *magnifying* the Lord. One meaning of that word is to glorify or exalt, but there's more. To magnify is also to make something bigger, just as you might study a map with a magnifying glass. Mary sings about the greatness of God and hopes his reputation will grow even greater.

In turn, the rest of the song deals with how God "magnifies" his people. In the first few verses, Mary sings about her own situation. God has chosen a lowly servant girl from Galilee and has done great things for her. As a result, she says, "all generations will call me blessed"—a prophecy that is still being fulfilled today. But she is not bragging. Mary knows she's a nobody who has been selected for a special honor.

The next section of the Magnificat expands the focus. Not only has God done this amazing thing for Mary, but he does this sort of thing all the time. He lifts the lowly and topples the mighty. When people show pride, he humbles them. When people humbly honor him, he exalts them.

This theme parallels much of Jesus' preaching in later years. He told his disciples, for instance, to avoid taking the seat of honor at a banquet. Better to be bumped up to a nicer seat than demoted. "For all who exalt themselves will be humbled, and those who humble themselves will be exalted" (Luke 14:11). The kingdom of God, he often preached, is an upside-down place, full of surprises. The people who think they have it made don't. Prostitutes and tax collectors will get to God's kingdom before the religious leaders. Why? Because they are humble enough to accept the grace God offered.

It's interesting to see that Mary, with Jesus still in her womb, was already in tune with him. We can only wonder how much Jesus' ideas were shaped by Mary as he grew up.

In the final verses of this prayer, Mary focuses on the nation of Israel. Her child was the Messiah, the promised deliverer. She could have chosen any number of messianic prophecies from the Hebrew Scriptures, but she went back to the beginning of the Jewish nation. On several occasions, God had spoken to Abraham, promising that he would become the father of a great nation. That promise had come true; the nation of Israel had developed and flourished. But God also told him, "In you all families of the earth shall be blessed" (Genesis 12:3).

This is, no doubt, the prophecy Mary has in mind. She knew the Messiah's kingdom would break through national boundaries. It would include Jews and people of all nations. As the elderly watchman Simeon prayed eight days after Jesus' birth, this child would become "a light for revelation to the Gentiles and for glory to your people Israel" (Luke 2:32).

You might expect a young woman to be in shock over the news of a virgin birth. You might expect Mary to focus on her own needs at such a time. But in this prayer she sees the big picture. She turns her magnifying glass on these events and shows that this isn't just a young woman's miraculous pregnancy in an obscure village near Galilee. God is doing that topsy-turvy thing he always does, and he is lighting a torch in Israel that will enlighten the whole world.

Mary was certainly an extraordinary woman, but it's because of what God enabled her to do. Her message is that God uses ordinary folks to do extraordinary things. Princes are toppled, and common people like Mary and like us are raised up for God's work. Feel incapable of doing what God wants? Join the club. But it's God's power, not yours, that will accomplish great things through you.

How to Pray the Magnificat

Pray this when God has done something great for you. Since God is regularly in that habit, you will have plenty of opportunities to pray it.

1. Begin by praising and rejoicing in the Lord. Let God know how great you think he is.

2. Focus on what God's recent actions have meant in your life. What specifically has he done for you? (Remind yourself that you don't deserve his kindness to you. This is about his greatness, not yours.)

3. Turn up the magnification level and think about how these events fit into the pattern of God's work in the world. What have you learned about God's nature in this process?

4. There are many promises in Scripture. See if God is fulfilling any of them in your life.

HOW MAJESTIC!
Psalm 8

O LORD, our Sovereign, how majestic is your name in all the earth! You have set your glory above the heavens. Out of the mouths of babes and infants you have founded a bulwark because of your foes, to silence the enemy and the avenger. When I look at your heavens, the work of your fingers, the moon and the stars that you have established; what are human beings that you are mindful of them, mortals that you care for them? Yet you have made them a little lower than God, and crowned them with glory and honor. You have given them dominion over the works of your hands; you have put all things under their feet, all sheep and oxen, and also the beasts of the field, the birds of the air, and the fish of the sea, whatever passes along the paths of the seas. O Lord, our Sovereign, how majestic is your name in all the earth.

Marveling at God's Creation

SOMETIMES THE glory of creation takes your breath away. Maybe it's a sunset that paints across the sky colors you've never seen before. Maybe it's a tranquil lake on a summer afternoon. It could be a dappled butterfly dancing on air above a rose in bloom, or a glistening horse in full gallop, or the inky expanse of the night sky flecked with stars. Scientists have explanations for each of these. They can tell you why we see colors at dusk and how a butterfly stays aloft. And they have plenty of theories about that starry night sky. But in those breathless moments, we recognize something that goes beyond all science. There is a Creator, and he is awesome.

The psalmist finds himself in such a moment as he prays the prayer of Psalm 8. The writing is credited to David, and we might imagine him in his youth, tending sheep on a Bethlehem hillside, gazing up at the moon and stars, and wondering about the God who put them there.

Yet the main point of this psalm is not the glory of creation but the amazing status of human beings. See how the song unfolds. It first asks the breath-catching question: In view of the glories of all God has made, *who are we?* How can you, God, possibly care about us when you've got all those stars to light up? We do seem awfully insignificant.

We can surely relate to that mind-set, but the psalm turns a corner, answering the question in a surprising way. Somehow, God doesn't consider us insignificant at all. He has crowned us with glory and honor, giving us a place of honor second only to himself. The creatures we marvel at are under our dominion. (This is clearly a reference to Genesis 1:28, where the first humans are given charge over the earth.)

In the movie *Big*, a boy gets his wish to be "bigger" and instantly becomes an adult. He lands a job as an executive in a toy company. Throughout the film, we see the adult business world through this youngster's eyes. He often has an attitude of "I can't believe I'm actually in charge of stuff!" That's somewhat the attitude we find in Psalm 8. "We're a bunch of nobodies, but look at what God has done for us."

That brings us back to that strange verse 2. Even the experts aren't sure about the meaning, but it seems as if the psalmist pictures God building a heavenly fortress out of the praises of "babes and infants." This leaves his enemies dumbfounded.

God keeps surprising us. He creates a magnificent world that makes us feel small, but then he puts us in charge of it and loves us endlessly. Jesus once said that God has counted every hair on our heads. Surely he has better things to do than that! But no, that's how much he cares for us. What are human beings? Fallible, yes. Sinful, yes. Disappointing, often. But still we are surprisingly loved and honored by our awesome Creator.

How to Pray the Majestic Prayer

1. Go out and look at the night sky—or any aspect of God's creation that inspires you.

2. Pray Psalm 8, and marvel at what God has made.

3. Instead of feeling insignificant, consider the ways that he has honored you. Thank him again for this surprise.

GREAT IS THY FAITHFULNESS
Lamentations 3:22–24

THE STEADFAST love of the LORD never ceases, his mercies never come to an end; they are new every morning; great is your faithfulness. "The Lord is my portion," says my soul, "therefore I will hope in him."

GOD'S LOVE AMONG THE RUINS

YOU WOULDN'T expect to find such a strong note of hope in a book called Lamentations. The prophet Jeremiah had plenty to lament about. The city of Jerusalem had been overrun by the fierce Babylonian army. Many people had been carted off to captivity. The Temple had been torn down and its treasures looted. As he began this book, the prophet pictured Jerusalem as a lonely widow, weeping all night long.

What made it worse for Jeremiah was that he knew exactly why this had happened. The people had turned away from the Lord. Jeremiah himself had delivered God's message of doom again and again, but the people had just laughed it off. God would never let his own Temple be destroyed, would he?

Yes, he would. He did. And Jeremiah saw it coming.

The prophet escaped to Egypt during the Babylonian onslaught, but sometime later he wandered back to the holy city, poking through the ruins. "Look and see if there is any sorrow like my sorrow," he wrote (Lamentations 1:12).

Halfway through this book of mourning, however, Jeremiah remembered something. Moments after saying, "I have forgotten what happiness is" (Lamentations 3:17), he added, "But this I call to mind, and therefore I have hope." That leads us into this prayer.

MOURNING TO MORNING

IT DOESN'T start like a prayer, but rather Jeremiah offers new insight about the Lord's love. But then he addresses God directly: Great is *your* faithfulness. It's easy to imagine the prophet sifting through the ashes and forgetting about God. In fact, in the earlier chapters he mentioned that there was no one around to offer comfort. But then this ray of hope peeks through, like the first hint of dawn. You, Lord! You are still here with us!

You can almost hear the gears shifting in the prophet's brain. *God has judged us, but he never stopped loving us. He promised destruction if the people refused to repent, and that did happen, but he's been loving us all the way through. This tragedy isn't a failure of God's love; it's a failure of our ability to obey him. His love is steadfast. His faithfulness is great. If we turn back to him now in our misery, he will help us put things back together!*

God's mercies are new every morning. What would it be like to be a producer on a morning talk show, with the challenge of coming up with exciting new material for each day? That's what God does. Every day he's looking for a different way to show his love for us. For Jeremiah, this newness was especially important. He—and his city—needed a new start. One of the first big "disaster movies," *The Poseidon Adventure,* became famous for a hit song that played at the end, "The Morning After." That's where Jeremiah was. The disaster had struck; now he needed a "morning after" in which the Lord would offer new mercies.

"The Lord is my portion," says Jeremiah. That's an interesting word that means just what you think it does. Mom carves up the casserole, and Sally gets this portion, and Billy gets this portion, and Jeremiah gets…the Lord. At the reading of the will, the wife gets the mansion and the cars, the son gets the trust fund, and Jeremiah gets…the Lord. The whole point is: the Lord is enough for him. The city had nothing left, but if the people accepted the portion that they still had—the Lord—they could renew their hope and get on with their lives.

The same is true for us. Disasters happen in our lives. It's tempting to spend a lot of time evaluating why they happened. Did we bring it on ourselves, or did someone else mess up? And why would God allow suffering anyway? Jeremiah doesn't invite us into that debate.

He just points to the dawning of God's new mercies. This is our portion, the steadfast love of God, and that is enough for us. So pick up a brick; it's time to start building anew.

HOW TO PRAY THE PRAYER OF NEW MERCIES

This prayer is designed for times of difficulty. Often we focus on our trials so much that we give them the power to destroy us. But when we turn our focus to God, our problems are put in perspective. That allows us to have hope.

1. Take 60 seconds to review your troubles—just 60 seconds. (Jeremiah took 64 verses before he turned the corner of hope.) Tell God what's wrong with your situation. Get your complaints out in the open, but then stop. For the rest of this prayer time, don't focus on your troubles.

2. Read the prayer out loud.

3. Think of something good that has happened to you today, some gift that God in his mercy brought you. Even if it's early in the day—the sun rose, didn't it? Thank him for this goodness.

4. Allow yourself to think of other ways God has shown his steadfast love and faithfulness to you.

5. Envision how hope in his faithfulness will transform your life through the coming week.

CHAPTER FIVE

PRAYERS *of* QUESTIONING

GIVE AND TAKE
Job 1:21

NAKED I CAME from my mother's womb, and naked shall I return there; the Lord gave, and the Lord has taken away; blessed be the name of the Lord.

GOD IS IN CONTROL

JOB WAS living the good life—vast wealth, a loving family, a good reputation, and a commitment to God. This man had it all. Many of the rich people in Scripture are seen as wicked, self-centered, and ignorant of the matters of the soul. Not Job. We're told he was "blameless and upright" (Job 1:1). His seven sons and three daughters would take turns throwing parties, and after each one, he would perform sacrifices on their behalf, just in case there had been any sins committed at those gatherings.

Then the roof fell in—literally. Not only did marauding enemies carry off his herds and kill his servants, but a storm knocked the roof off the house where Job's children were feasting. They were all killed.

Suddenly this rich man was poor. He had nothing left. No flocks. No home. No family, nothing except a complaining wife. And, since everyone assumed that Job must have sinned greatly to cause God to unleash such calamity, he didn't have much of a reputation left, either. How did Job respond to such tragedy? He tore his robes and shaved his head—both ancient eastern ways of showing grief—and then he "fell on the ground and worshiped" (Job 1:20). The Hebrew word for worship can refer to a respectful bow before any superior, but it often means falling prostrate before God. In this case Job, mourning deeply, opened his heart to God and prayed this famous prayer.

In 29 words (15 in Hebrew), he set forth a basic philosophy of suffering. Yes, God may rob us of the pleasures we have come to enjoy, but didn't he give them to us origi-

nally? How can we blame him for suffering unless we also credit him with joy? He doesn't owe us anything.

Job's wife couldn't understand. As the woes of Job continued and he developed sores all over his body, she urged him to "curse God, and die!" His response: "Shall we receive the good at the hand of God, and not receive the bad?"

As Job sat on the ash heap, three friends came to counsel him. They didn't seem to get it, either. They were sure that Job had sinned greatly, bringing these troubles upon himself. Then another friend, Elihu, arrived and said, basically, "God is God. He can do what he wants." God himself later confirmed this.

And that point is pretty close to Job's original prayer: "...the Lord gave and the Lord has taken away; blessed be the name of the Lord."

THE ZERO-SUM GAME

IN THE musical *My Fair Lady,* Professor Henry Higgins bets a friend that he can take a common flower girl from the street and make her a proper lady. He selects Eliza Doolittle and gives her a new wardrobe as well as lessons in speaking proper English. After a successful visit to the racetrack with his upper-crust friends, the professor tells Eliza that the bet has been won, the experiment is over, and she should go home.

This is a jolt to Eliza. She has grown accustomed to her life in the professor's home, attended by servants, wearing the finest gowns and jewels. Now she must leave all that behind. As she scolds him for being so callous, he wonders what the problem is. When he took her under his wing, she had nothing. Shouldn't she be grateful for what he had given her? Wasn't it his right to end the experiment?

Technically, he's right. And that's the point that Job accepts in his prayer. He began life with nothing, and he'll end it in the same way. Whatever he owns he has received from God. God has every right to take it away. In fact, the book of Job lets us know that the calamities that came upon Job were the result of a wager between God and the devil. Would Job remain faithful to God even when everything was taken away? God, like Higgins, was conducting a human experiment.

But there's a greater issue involved, beyond Job's suffering. *My Fair Lady* shows that the professor and the girl become fond of each other. Higgins has a right to end the experiment, but Eliza wants a *relationship*. The same issue underlies the story of Job. Had the book tried to explain why people suffer, it would have done a pretty poor job of it. But it's not about that. It's about Job's relationship with God. Bad things happen, and Job is faithful. His wife wants him to forget about God, but he will not. His friends belittle him, but he insists, "I know that my Redeemer lives" (Job 19:25). He trusts God through the calamity. Almost as an afterthought, God restores all that Job lost. It was never about his riches. It was Job's faith that won the wager. He continued to bless the name of the Lord.

Bad things have happened to you, no doubt. And, just as Job's friends did, you've tried to figure out why. A loving God would treat you better, wouldn't he? There's plenty of deep thinking you can do on that subject, but don't miss the simple wisdom of Job's prayer. God gives and he takes, but through it all he is there. Don't just thank God for what he has given you. Bless him for who he is.

HOW TO PRAY THE PRAYER OF JOB

1. Admit your pain. It may sound obvious, but many believers have a hard time with this. They sugarcoat life and deny that they're suffering. Job was honest about his hurt.

2. Think about the good things God has done for you as well as the bad things that have happened. Try to get a full picture of the give-and-take of your life.

3. Agree that God has the right to do anything. He doesn't owe you any of the finer things in life.

4. Renew your relationship with God. Bless his name. Express your commitment to God, even though you may not understand what he's doing. He may take away all you have, but his greatest gift endures—the gift of himself.

HERE AM I,
SEND SOMEONE ELSE
Exodus 4:13

O MY LORD, please send someone else.

ALLOWING GOD TO USE US

ONE OF THE great things about the Bible is its honesty. You might expect a religious book to say only good things about the religious people it portrays. But the Bible shows us the foibles of its main characters. Noah, Abraham and Sarah, Moses, David, Solomon, Elijah—none of these portrayals is spotless. They are shown as real people, with the same doubts, fears, and passions as anyone else.

Moses was possibly the most esteemed figure in Israelite history. After all, he stood up to the mighty Pharaoh of Egypt, demanding "Let my people go!" But how he got to that point—well, the details are less than heroic.

The Israelites worked as slaves in Egypt. Fearing a population boom among these workers, the Egyptians began killing all boys born to the Israelites. Moses' mother saved her son by placing him in a basket of bulrushes and floating him down the river, where he was found by Pharaoh's daughter. She adopted little Moses as her own. Moses was reared in Pharaoh's court and accorded the finest education available. But one day a grown-up Moses saw a taskmaster abusing an Israelite slave. After killing the taskmaster, Moses fled into the desert, a fugitive from justice.

In the Sinai desert he made a decent living as a nomadic shepherd, but then an odd sight grabbed his attention. A bush was burning but was not being consumed by the flames. Moses approached it and heard the voice of God.

The Lord said he knew about his people's suffering in Egypt. He wanted to set them free and lead them to a new land. He needed Moses to deliver his message to Pharaoh.

Let's step back a moment and consider the whole breadth of Scripture. God often asks people to do things, and we often hear them

responding in faith and obedience. God asks Noah to build an ark, and he does. Young Samuel responds to God's voice with "Speak, Lord, I'm listening." Isaiah has a vision of God in the Temple asking "Whom shall I send?" The prophet responds, "Here am I; send me!"

That's not exactly what we get from Moses.

First he stammers, "Who am I?" He's nobody special, and yet God is asking him to do a great thing. God replies that it doesn't matter: "I will be with you."

Moses worries that the Israelites won't even believe God sent him, so God gives him his own name as a calling card—I AM WHO I AM.

Moses isn't buying it: "What if they still don't believe me?" he asks. God gives him miraculous tricks to perform: turning his staff into a snake, making his hand white with leprosy, changing water to blood.

But there's another protest from Moses. "O my Lord, I have never been eloquent,...I am slow of speech and slow of tongue." God points out that he created Moses' tongue. "I will...teach you what you are to speak."

All out of excuses, Moses cries out his prayer: "Please send someone else!" Finally the Lord gets upset with Moses, but he agrees to send Moses' brother, Aaron, as a spokesman.

SECRET SERVICE

WE'RE BEING a bit tough on Moses here, but only because we've all been there. We live our lives in comfort zones, but sometimes we get a sense that God wants us to try something new. Perhaps you might teach a fifth-grade Sunday school class, invite a neighbor to your small-group Bible study, or make friends with the coworker who just moved here from another state or country.

And we tend to trot out all of Moses' excuses. Who am I, Lord? Nobody! I don't have the talents required. You need a professional for that. I love you, Lord, but don't ask me to do that. Send someone else.

If you've prayed this particular prayer of Moses lately, don't feel guilty. You're in good company. But understand that, when you run out of excuses, that bush will still be burning, and the voice will still be calling. If you let God lead you on a new adventure, you might be surprised at what he can do through you.

Amazingly, God used Moses to do mighty things in spite of all his excuses. He confronted the Pharaoh, supported by his brother Aaron, and he led his people out of slavery. He became the nation's greatest leader but not because he wanted to be. He simply allowed the Lord to push him out of his comfort zone. Let God do the same for you.

REWORKING THE PRAYER OF MOSES

1. Look out for "burning bushes." Keep your eyes open for ways that God is trying to get your attention.

2. Don't focus on your own ability or inability. Consider how God will give you power to do what he wants you to do.

3. Ask for help if you need it. God can give you the talents you need, but he can also give you talented people to support you.

CHAPTER SIX

PRAYERS *of* REPENTANCE *and* RECOMMITMENT

A KING'S CONFESSION
Psalm 51:1–17

Have mercy on me, O God, according to your steadfast love; according to your abundant mercy blot out my transgressions. Wash me thoroughly from my iniquity, and cleanse me from my sin.

For I know my transgressions, and my sin is ever before me. Against you, you alone, have I sinned, and done what is evil in your sight, so that you are justified in your sentence and blameless when you pass judgment. Indeed, I was born guilty, a sinner when my mother conceived me.

You desire truth in the inward being; therefore teach me wisdom in my secret heart. Purge me with hyssop, and I shall be clean; wash me, and I shall be whiter than snow. Let me hear joy and gladness; let the bones that you have crushed rejoice. Hide your face from my sins, and blot out all my iniquities.

Create in me a clean heart, O God, and put a new and right spirit within me. Do not cast me away from your presence, and do not take your holy spirit from me. Restore to me the joy of your salvation, and sustain in me a willing spirit.

Then I will teach transgressors your ways, and sinners will return to you. Deliver me from bloodshed, O God, O God of my salvation, and my tongue will sing aloud of your deliverance.

O Lord, open my lips, and my mouth will declare your praise. For you have no delight in sacrifice; if I were to give a burnt offering, you would not be pleased. The sacrifice acceptable to God is a broken spirit; a broken and contrite heart, O God, you will not despise.

A PSALM OF SORROW FOR SIN

THE KING had committed adultery. In his attempt to hide his sin, he had the woman's husband killed. In most nations, this wouldn't have been a problem. Kings let their lusts run freely. But in Israel, the king didn't call the shots—God did. So when the prophet Nathan confronted King David with his sin, the king knew he had to repent publicly (2 Samuel 11–12).

It had started on a flat rooftop as David strolled there, probably to cool off in the evening. He spied Bathsheba bathing on a rooftop across the way, and he wanted her. The king sent for her and slept with her, and she became pregnant. Since her husband was off fighting in the army, it would be plain to all that the birth was illegitimate. The shame would eventually make its way back to David.

So he attempted a cover-up worthy of modern politics. Calling the husband back from battle, the king rewarded him for his good service, offering him some time with his wife. Then people would think the child-to-be belonged to the husband. A great plan—except the loyal soldier refused to enjoy his wife's company while his fellow soldiers were still in battle. The husband slept outside the king's door. Finally David sent the husband back to the front lines with a secret message for the general: Get into fierce fighting and pull back. In other words, *Make sure this man dies.*

The plan worked. In a magnanimous gesture, King David married the widow of this war hero and offered to raise the child as his own. What a great monarch! As far as anyone knew, David was a paragon of virtue in this matter. But God knew otherwise, and he sent the prophet Nathan to David with a parable.

There was a situation the king needed to know about, said the prophet. A rich man with many flocks, desiring the only lamb of his poor neighbor, stole that lamb and ate it for dinner. Hearing this, David was livid. How could such injustice occur in his kingdom? "That man deserves to die!" the king raged.

"You are the man," Nathan replied, and David was cut to the quick. God struck the newborn baby with a deadly illness, leading David to begin a very public repentance, fasting and throwing himself on the ground. David begged God to spare the child's life, but the child died within a week.

Some time later, according to the title sentence attached to Psalm 51, David wrote his song of confession. It's an amazing cry of the heart, a plea for forgiveness. It's all the more remarkable because of the public nature of these words. The innermost feelings of Israel's king were being broadcast, printed up in the nation's hymnal. But as a result, this psalm has been used by countless believers as a model for their own repentance.

A NEED FOR CLEANSING

THIS PSALM has many descriptions of forgiveness, but most of them have to do with washing. Elsewhere David prays that his sins be "covered" (Psalm 32:1), but maybe at this time he's already had too much covering up. He needs something far more radical—a thorough cleansing inside and out.

Note also that the basis for forgiveness is God's own "steadfast love" and mercy. It's not that David's such a good guy or that he'll go on to do great things—God forgives sin because that is what he does. It's who he is.

This is something to remember as we come to God in repentance. Often in our human interactions we ask for forgiveness based on the triviality of the offense ("I didn't mean it") or our own general goodness ("I won't do it again"). Sometimes we even *demand* forgiveness because of our good track record ("After all I've done for you!"). But none of that is appropriate with God. He has every right to cast us away from his presence. But instead, because of his loving mercy, he cleans, washes, restores, and sustains.

Christian theologians are tantalized by a couple of points in this psalm. It seems to establish the idea of original sin, though it could also be David's poetic lament over his inability to do right. There is also the mention of the "holy spirit" of God—long before the New Testament developed the doctrine of the Trinity. And yet, isn't this basically the same idea—the ongoing, indwelling presence of God in the believer's life? Salvation is another New Testament concept that shows up here, though the Old Testament often shows God saving his people in various ways. Here David asks God to restore "the joy of [God's] salvation." This battle-scarred warrior had certainly experienced God's deliverance on many occasions. Is he praying for a spiritual deliverance here, or does he long for the joy that comes from knowing that God will once again be on his side, ready to help? Notice that the "joy of salvation" is placed parallel to

David's own willing spirit. As we pray this psalm, we might find the same parallel: We're on the same page with God; we eagerly participate in his plans for us.

Toward the end of this psalm, David promises to speak out about God and his ways. The time for secrecy is over. David will offer both praise to God and instruction to other sinners. As a result, people would "turn to God."

What God wants is our hearts. Are you truly sorry for your sins? Then pray the prayer of David, begging for forgiveness from a God who loves to show mercy.

How to Pray the Prayer of David

1. Be specific about the sin you're sorry for.

2. Throw yourself on God's mercy. Don't try to excuse yourself.

3. Make sure your religious observance is backed by a sincerely contrite heart.

4. Ask God to give you a "willing spirit" and the "joy of his salvation." See how you can participate fully in his plans for you.

5. Praise God vocally, and look for ways to tell others about God's forgiveness.

A SINNER'S PRAYER
Luke 18:13

GOD, BE merciful to me, a sinner!

GOD IS MERCIFUL

TAX COLLECTORS were a hated people in Jesus' day. First, they were traitors, collecting money from their fellow Jews on behalf of the despised Roman government. Second, they weren't nice about it at all. Tax collectors would charge extra to increase their own profit. If someone argued, the collectors could call in some thugs from the Roman army for some additional "persuasion." Tax collectors would take things from people's houses and beat those who could not pay—all with the veneer of legality and the protection of Rome. Because of their collaboration with the Romans, tax collectors were naturally shunned from the religious life of Israel. Because of their entanglements with "unclean" Gentiles, tax collectors had no chance of following Jewish law.

In the Gospels, we often find tax collectors lumped together with prostitutes. Together, these groups were the lowest of the low, rejected by proper society and morally scorned. As most people saw it, these sinners had given up any hope of a relationship with a holy God.

On the other hand, the Pharisees were a respected people in Jesus' day. They devoted their entire lives to understanding and keeping God's law to the letter. Pharisees sought God's favor as an eager student seeks a

teacher's approval. They were the first to answer the tough religious questions, their behavior was impeccable, and they were always sure to let everyone know how well they knew God.

Officially, their hope was to usher in the Messiah's arrival by making the nation completely righteous. To do this, they even added extra laws to God's laws. They wanted to "build a hedge" around the scriptural commands so that people wouldn't even come close to breaking them. Pharisees were experts in holiness, the upper crust in this very religious society.

HUMBLE HEARTS ARE HEARD IN HEAVEN

BUT JESUS had a way of turning everything around. He told a simple story of two people going to the temple to pray—a Pharisee and a tax collector. Jesus' listeners would wonder what a tax collector was doing anywhere close to the temple. The Pharisee belonged there, but the tax collector didn't.

In Jesus' story, the Pharisee prays first, boasting about his own religious achievements. He thanks God that he is not as sinful as others—like that tax collector standing over there.

The tax collector had a completely different attitude. He was "standing far off." Standing was the common posture for prayer, but the Pharisee had taken center stage while the tax collector tried to melt into the scenery. This humble sinner would not even look up toward heaven, as most people did in prayer; he beat his chest as a sign of despair and uttered this basic prayer.

Try to put yourself in the crowd of Jesus' listeners. Tax collectors have taken your money, but Pharisees, while they can be arrogant, seem to be good people. As you hear this tax collector in Jesus' story asking for mercy, your reaction might be: "After all you've done, how dare you ask for mercy!" And then you hear the conclusion of the story. It was the tax collector, Jesus said, who went home justified before God, not the Pharisee. Jesus shocks us by showing that God exalts the ultimate sinner who is humble while he humbles the epitome of righteousness who is proud.

The Pharisees may have meant well, but somewhere along the way their knowledge replaced God's revelations, their good behavior replaced their genuine love for their neighbor, and their desire for worldly status replaced their desire to be servants of God. With all the praise they received from others (and from themselves), they no longer saw themselves as sinners. There's nothing wrong with trying to live a good life. The problem comes when we forget our weaknesses. The Bible tells us that "all have sinned and fall short of the glory of God" (Romans 3:23). God can work with us only when we recognize that we are included in the "all" of this verse.

Maybe you know someone who is "cleanliness-challenged." Such people might want to clean a room, but they have a hard time even seeing the dirt that's there. One apartment-dweller might run a rag over a counter and say it is clean, but a roommate comes along and says, "It's still filthy!" It's not a lack of effort; it's a lack of *seeing*.

In the same way, it's only when we recognize our sins that we can repent for them. The Pharisees were blind to the dirt in their souls. They needed God's mercy, too, but they didn't know enough to ask for it. The tax collector recognized his sin and his need for mercy. So should we.

HOW TO PRAY THE SINNER'S PRAYER

1. Do not think too highly of your righteousness. Remember that we all have sinned.

2. Come to the Lord with humility and a repentant heart.

3. Be honest with God, never hiding your sins from him.

4. Memorize this short prayer, and utter it throughout your day.